Stephanie Jones

Illustrations by Blueberry Illustrations

To my daughter Daisy,

and my husband Christopher.
You have been my inspiration and support.

There's a little girl named Daisy May.

She must wear an
eye patch every day.

In her one little eye, there's a little white spot.

Daisy thought she could see fine... but the doctor did not.

Daisy cried, "This patch
is hurting my sight…"

"With only one eye, I can't see just right!"

She hated the patch—
it was such a bother.
She tore it in two in
front of her father.

Her mother still covered her eye each day. Daisy would pull it off and say, "No way!"

No matter how much she whined or how much she cried, "You still have to wear it," her mother sighed.

Her big sister didn't
have a patch to wear.
Miss Daisy didn't
think that was fair.

"She looks like a pirate!" her big sister said.

"If Daisy will share it…
I'll wear it instead!"

Mother said,
"You can't wear a
patch just because
Daisy has one."

"You can't wear a patch… even if it looks fun."

Daisy thought, *If my Big Sister wants it, maybe it's not so bad...*

...maybe I'll wear it today, just to make her so mad!

Then one day Daisy forgot she had the patch on.
Accidentally she wore it all the day long!

Her mother was happy,
as was her father.
It made little Daisy think
it was worth all the bother.

So she wore a patch again
the very next day…

…and she knew in her heart,
"This fits Daisy May!"